Collins Primary S

HOUSES AND HOMES

Linda Howe

Resources Needed

Collections To Be Made

Building materials (2, 8, 14)

Pictures of different homes (3, 4)

Books about homes (4)

Window cleaning sprays and liquids (7)

General Resources

Building toys (1)

Paper (2, 4, 13)

Bag/box (2)

Crayons (2, 3, 4, 12)

Unifix blocks/counters (3)

Squared paper (3)

Glue (4, 11, 12, 13)

Scissors (4, 6, 8, 11, 13)

Lego (5, 10)

Plasticine (5)

Card (5, 6, 9, 10, 12)

Plastic farm and zoo animals (5)

Art straws (6)

Pipe cleaners (6, 11)

Garden cane (6)

String (6, 11)

Sticky tape (6, 9, 11, 12)

Newspaper (7)

Cloths (7)

Heavy objects (9)

Pencils (13)

Lolly sticks (8)

Cardboard boxes (10, 12)

Foil/plastic (10)

Plastic bottles (10)

Plastic straws (11)

Fabric pieces (11, 12)

Cardboard tubes (12)

Paint (12)

Coloured paper (12)

Magazines and catalogues (13)

Bowl of water (14)

Hammers (14)

Plastic bags (14)

Sandpaper (14)

Other Resources

Mirror tiles (7)

Contents

	Resources needed	2
1	Shapes of buildings	4
2	Exploring building materials	6
3	Where do you live?	8
4	Sets of houses	10
5	Who lives here?	12
6	Tall buildings	14
7	Helping at home	16
8	Scratch tests	18
9	Which shape tower is strongest?	20
10	Homes in different places	22
11	Tents	24
12	Designing a house	26
13	What is inside a house?	28
14	Strong houses	30
	Acknowledgements	32

1 SHAPES OF BUILDINGS

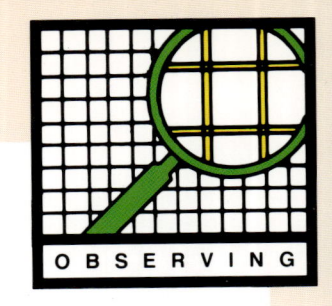

OBSERVING

What shapes are buildings?
Think about:

blocks of flats    detached houses    semi-detached houses    bungalows

castles    terraced houses    churches

What other buildings can you think of?
You might be able to go for a walk near your school to see how many different shaped buildings you can see.

Think about windows.
What shape are the school windows? They might be:

round   square   rectangular   oval   arched   pointed

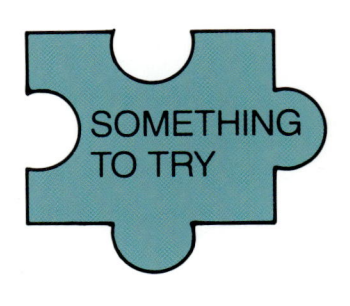

SOMETHING TO TRY

Take a piece of coloured paper and some charcoal or chalks. Draw some shapes of buildings. You only need to draw the outlines.

Now draw in the windows. How many different shaped windows can you draw?

Think about roofs.
Some houses have flat roofs, some have sloping roofs and some have pointed roofs.
What kind of roof does your home have?

What shapes are buildings?

YOU NEED Different building toys

ACTIVITY -A- How many different shaped buildings can you make?
Are some toys easier to build with than others?
Which building stands tallest?

ACTIVITY -B- Choose one kind of toy. Take some building pieces and count how many you have.
How many different buildings can you make using just those pieces?

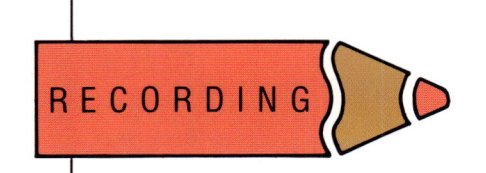

RECORDING You can draw the buildings you have made and put them on display.

2 EXPLORING BUILDING MATERIALS

OBSERVING

Finding out about different building materials

YOU NEED
A collection of building materials
Paper   A bag or box   Crayons

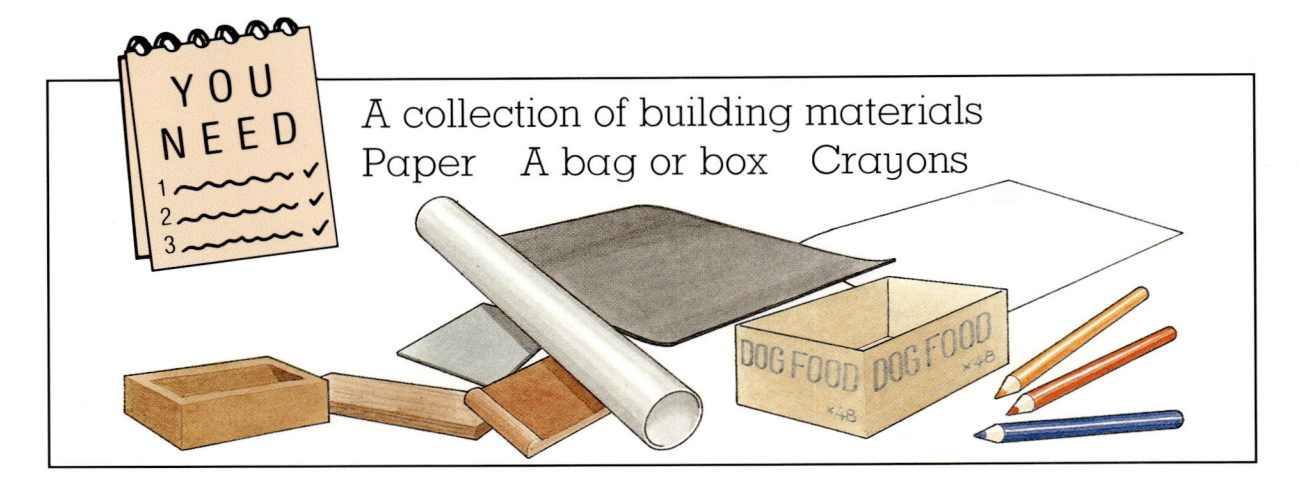

ACTIVITY -A-

Look at and feel the building materials. Choose one to look at closely.

Is it:
- hard or soft?
- heavy or light?
- rough or smooth?
- warm or cold?
- crumbly?
- bendy?

- Does it have straight or wavy edges?
- What shape is it?
- What colour is it? What else can you say about it?

Look closely at another material. In what ways is it the same? How is it different?

RECORDING

Draw one of the building materials and write words around it that describe it.

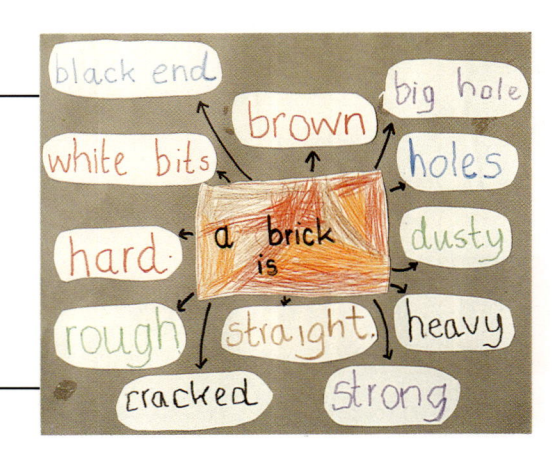

a brick is: black end, brown, big hole, white bits, holes, hard, dusty, rough, straight, heavy, cracked, strong

ACTIVITY -B- Choose one of the building materials and use the paper and crayons to make a rubbing. You may have to wrap the material in the paper to hold it still. Now put the material in a bag or box and put your rubbing next to it. Can another group or a friend guess what is in the bag or box by looking at your rubbing?

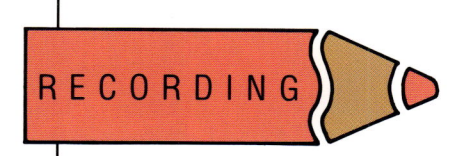

RECORDING You can put the rubbings into books or folders.

ACTIVITY -C-

Put all the building materials on a table. With a group of children stand around the table facing away from it so that none of you can see the things on the table. One child should turn round and tap the table with one of the materials. Can you guess which material they used? Do all the materials make the same sound?

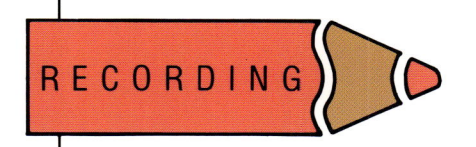

RECORDING Make a tape recording of the sounds you made.

WHERE DO YOU LIVE?

Can you tell a story about living in an unusual place?
It might be:

a windmill

a round house

a tree house

a lighthouse

Can you find pictures of different homes in books and magazines?
Which house is the most like the one you live in?

Draw a picture of your home or make a model of it.

Is there anyone else in the class who lives in a home that looks like yours?
How is your home different from other people's?
You may be able to bring a photograph of your home to school.

Can you make a chart to show where everyone in the class lives?

YOU NEED

Unifix blocks or counters   Crayons
Squared paper   Pictures of different homes

ACTIVITY

Choose one colour of block or counter for each kind of home, like this:
- flats – green
- mobile homes – blue
- bungalows – red
- terraces – yellow

You don't have to use these colours. You can choose your own.

Talk about which children in your class live in each kind of home. Each of you can take a block in the colour that shows the kind of home you live in.

Which kind of home has the most blocks?

RECORDING

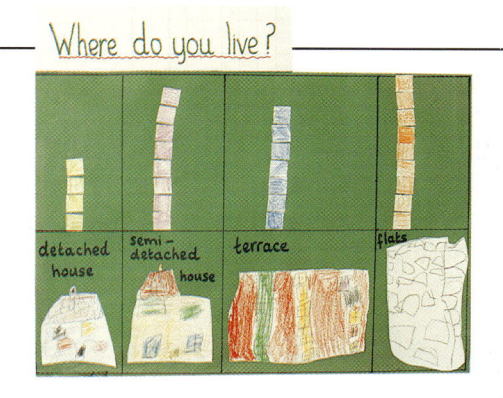

Use squared paper and pictures of homes to make a chart to show what you have found out. Colour in a square for each block.
Write numbers at the sides of the chart to make it easy to read. Where do most children live?
Where do fewest children live?

SETS OF HOUSES

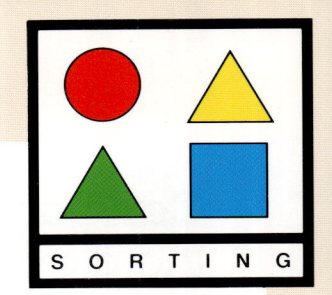

SORTING

Some of the first people on earth probably made homes in caves. What do you think it would be like to live in a cave? Would it be:
- warm?
- comfortable?
- light?

Some people live in homes which can be moved, like tents and caravans.
What would you need to take with you if you moved to a new home?

Sometimes people have moved buildings by taking down each brick and putting a number on it. They use the numbers to help to put the buildings back together as they were.

SOMETHING TO FIND OUT

Make a Lego house. When you have built it take your house to bits and try and build it again in just the same way. Is your new house exactly the same as your first house?

Finding out about different homes

YOU NEED
Magazine pictures of houses   Glue
Books about homes   Paper   Scissors
Crayons

ACTIVITY

Cut out pictures of homes from magazines or copy some from books.
Use the pictures to make some sets. You could try:
- homes like yours and homes not like yours
- homes built using different things
- homes that you see in our country and homes that you see in other countries
- modern and old homes
- homes from hot, cold, wet and dry places
- homes which can move and homes which cannot

What other sets could you make?

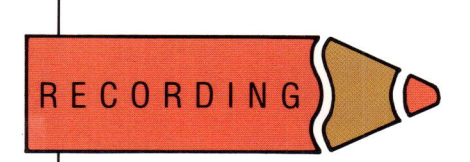

RECORDING

You can stick some of the sets on paper to make a record.

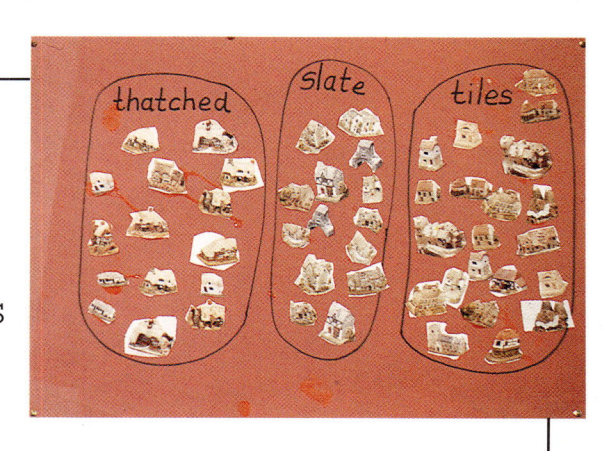

WHO LIVES HERE?

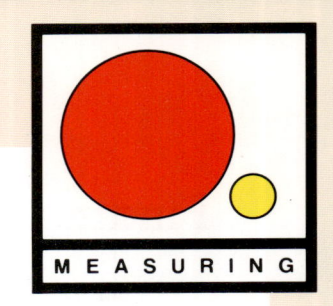

What kinds of homes do animals live in?
What might live in:

a hole?    a nest?    the jungle?

a tree    a desert?    the water?

What kinds of creatures live in:
- our country?
- cold countries?
- warm countries?

Do any pets share your home?
Where do they sleep?
What do you need to do to look after them?
Think of some creatures that you would not like in your home.
They might be too big, too noisy, too messy, or too rough.

Making homes for different creatures

YOU NEED: Plastic farm and zoo animals, Lego, Plasticine, Card

ACTIVITY -A-

Choose several different plastic animals. Choose some which are big, tall, small and short. Can you make a Lego house for:
- a tall animal like a giraffe?
- a big animal like an elephant?
- a small animal like a lamb?
- a short animal like a piglet?

Will the animals fit in the houses you have made?

ACTIVITY -B-

Use the Plasticine to make a long snake and a short snake.
Can you make card houses for each snake?
Do they fit inside?
Now make a medium-sized house.
Can you make a snake to fit inside it?

RECORDING

You could make a display of all the houses or take photographs of them. You could also make a drawing of a house for one of the animals.

TALL BUILDINGS

MEASURING

Can you think of some stories or rhymes about houses?
In *Hansel and Gretel* there is a house made of sweets.
Do you know the poem about the crooked man who lived in a crooked house?
In *Snow White* there is a house for dwarfs.
Can you find some more houses in stories or rhymes?
Draw a picture of one of them or of a house that you have imagined for yourself.

Do you have stairs in your house?
Some buildings are very tall. They have lifts to help you get to the top.
Some buildings have moving staircases called escalators.
Are there any stairs in your school?
Is there an upstairs?
How many stairs are there?
How do you think you would feel if you had to go to the top of a very tall building?
What might you see?

Can you make a tall building?

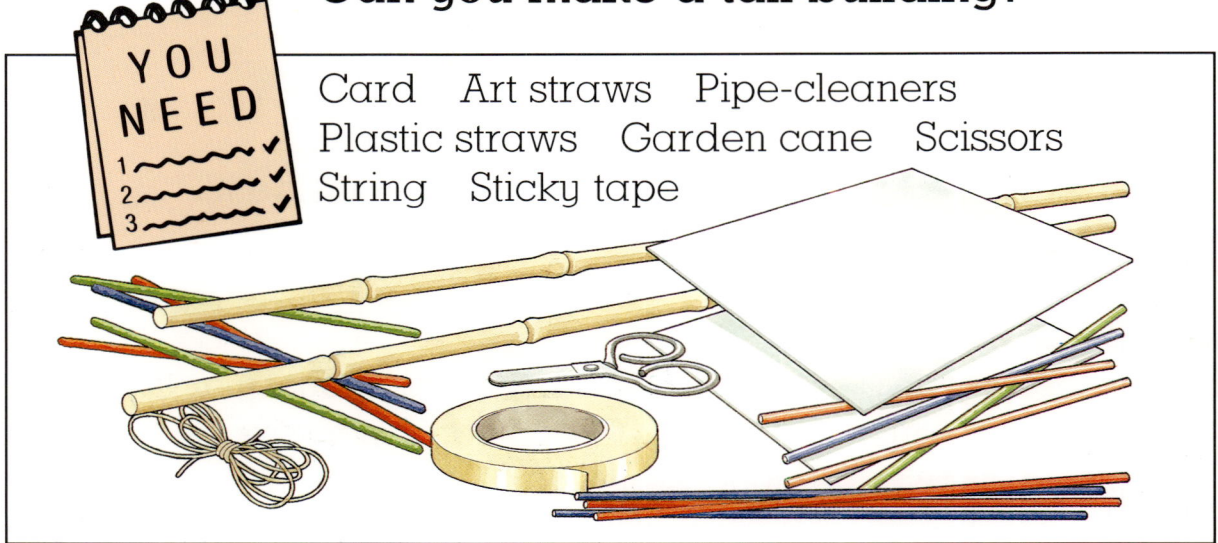

YOU NEED

Card   Art straws   Pipe-cleaners
Plastic straws   Garden cane   Scissors
String   Sticky tape

ACTIVITY

See who can build the tallest building just using the things listed.
The building must stand up by itself without falling over.
You can work by yourself or with a friend in a group.
Before you start think carefully about your building and plan it.
You might want to talk your ideas over with a friend and draw a picture of your plan.
When you have decided on your plan you can start making your building.
Whose building is the tallest?
Which building stands up best?
Could you make your building better in any way?

RECORDING

You could take photographs of the finished buildings.

7 HELPING AT HOME

Do you help at home?
Think about all the jobs that need to be done, such as:

cleaning    cooking    washing clothes

washing dishes    drying dishes    making beds

Can you think of any others?

Make a list of all the household jobs that you can think of.
You could make a written list or a picture list.
Put a cross next to any jobs that you help with.
Tick all the jobs that have to be done each day.
Draw a line under the jobs which only need doing once a week.

Think about cleaning.
How many different things need cleaning?
Think about:

- floors
- walls
- doors
- tables
- cookers
- windows
- mirrors
- ornaments

Can you think of any others?
What do we use to clean these things?
Do we use the same thing for cleaning everything?
What would happen if we used the wrong thing?
Suppose we used shoe polish to clean the windows?

Testing to find the best thing to clean windows with

YOU NEED: Mirror tiles   Newspaper   Soap and water   Window cleaning sprays and liquids   Cloths

ACTIVITY

Each group should have a mirror tile and a cloth. The tiles should be grubby or smeared. Each group can try to clean the mirror tiles in different ways. One group can use soap, water and newspaper as people once did. They washed with soap and water and rubbed with newspaper.

The other groups can each use a different kind of cleaner. Test to find out which group can make their tile the cleanest. How will you decide which tile is cleanest? Will you time your tests? How could you time them? Which cleaning method is best?

RECORDING

You could give a mark out of ten for each way of cleaning and this could be recorded on a chart.

What cleaned best?

ways we cleaned	marks out of ten
powder	6
liquid	10
spray	9
newspaper	2

SCRATCH TESTS

FAIR TESTING

What happens when things get scratched?
Have you ever had a new toy which has got scratched?
How did you feel?
Can you think of any ways to stop a new toy from getting scratched?

Look around your school.
Can you see any scratch marks?
There may be some on the walls, the doors or the tables.
Can you find any other places with scratches?
How could you stop them getting scratched?

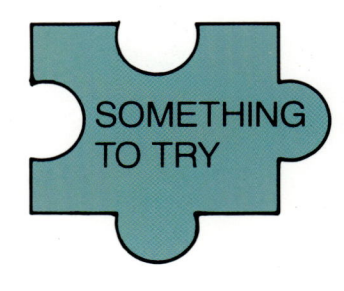

SOMETHING TO TRY

Use wax crayons to colour all over a piece of card.
Use a mixture of colours and colour thickly.
Go over the colours with a black crayon so that you cannot see any of the colours.
Choose something to scratch with. It could be the wrong end of a paint brush, a lolly stick or a plastic spoon.
Scratch a picture on the black and look at the colours showing through.

Testing to see which building materials are the easiest to scratch

YOU NEED

Building materials   Lolly sticks
Plastic spoons   Nails   1p and 2p pieces
Scissors

ACTIVITY

Put the things which can be used for scratching on the table so that you can look at them. You might use lolly sticks, 1p or 2p coins, plastic spoons, nails or open scissors.
Which do you think will be the easiest to scratch with?
Which will be the hardest?

Try putting the things in order.
First, choose the thing which you think is hardest to scratch with and try to scratch the different building materials with it.
Does it leave a mark on any of them?

Now take turns in using the other things to scratch with.
Which of them scratch the building materials?
Are there more scratches on some things than on others?

Which material would you use for a surface that gets scratched a lot?

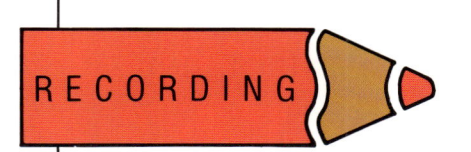

RECORDING

Make a chart to show the results. Draw scratches in the right boxes.

WHICH SHAPE TOWER IS STRONGEST?

Are there any castles near you? You might be able to visit one or find pictures of castles in books. What shapes are the different parts of a castle?

Early castles had a wooden building called a *keep* on top of a steep hill. There was a wooden fence around the keep called a *palisade*. Why do you think that wood was not the best material to use for castle building? Think about, strength, fire and rotting as well as other things.

People started to build castles of stone. Why do you think that stone might be a better building material?

The first stone keeps were square or rectangular. They were often built on hills or cliffs or river banks. Why do you think that these places were chosen?
Later, keeps were often round. Why do you think that they were round?

Can you find out the strongest shape for a tower?

YOU NEED Card   Sticky tape   Heavy objects

ACTIVITY -A-

Work with a group of friends to make towers. Before you begin each of you should choose a different shape to make. You could try:

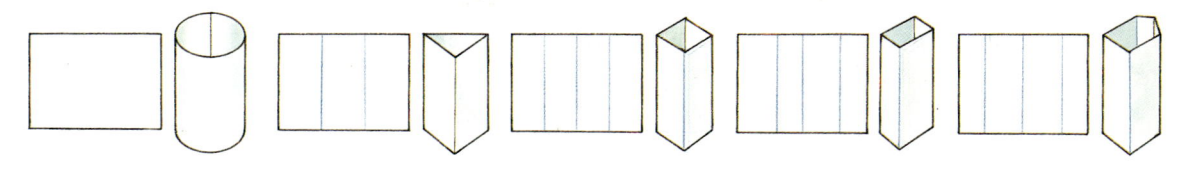

round   triangular   square   rectangular   house-shaped

or an idea of your own.
Make your towers.
Fold carefully so that they stand straight and stick them together using tape.

ACTIVITY -B-

How can you test the towers to see how strong they are? You could put heavy objects on top to see how many they will hold.
You could use weights or bricks or you might like to try an idea of your own.
Test your towers.
Which shape is strongest? Do other groups find the same?

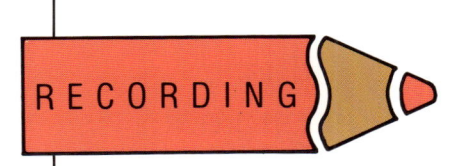

RECORDING

Make a chart to show what you discovered.

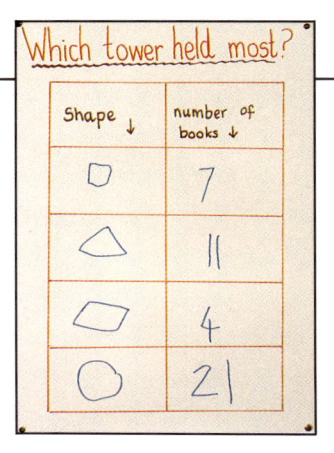

Which tower held most?

Shape ↓	number of books ↓
▢	7
△	11
▱	4
○	21

HOMES IN DIFFERENT PLACES

Can you find any pictures of houses in other countries? Look carefully at the roofs. Are they flat or sloping?

Why do you think that houses in hot, dry countries often have flat roofs?

This picture is of a house in a country where they have a lot of snow. It is a chalet in Switzerland. Why do you think that the roofs of chalets have a slope?

Think about some other countries and look at the roofs of their houses. You could write a story about what it might be like to live where it is wet, very hot or very snowy.

Finding out about different roofs

YOU NEED

Cardboard boxes   Card   Plasticine
Cooking foil or plastic   Lego   Plastic bottles with screwtops or a watering can.

ACTIVITY -A- Use the boxes to make some model houses with different shaped roofs. You could try:

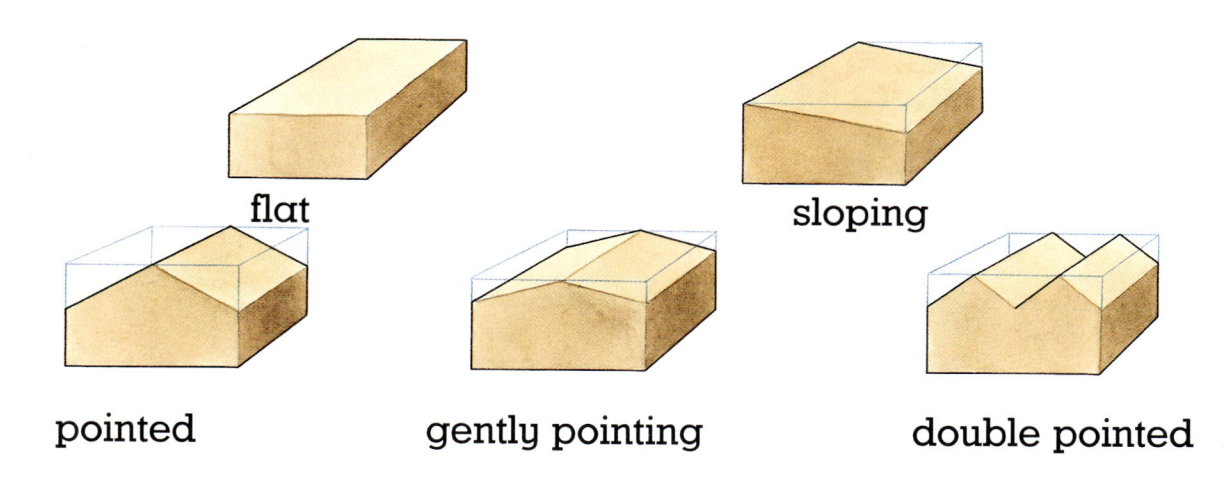

flat

sloping

pointed

gently pointing

double pointed

As well as ideas of your own.

Cover the roofs with either foil or plastic.
Try tipping some water on the roofs, using a watering can or plastic bottles with holes in the lids to make "rain". Does the water run off the roofs or does it make puddles?

ACTIVITY -B- Make some Plasticine or Lego houses with different roofs and try again.
Which roofs do you think are the best shapes for houses in wet countries?

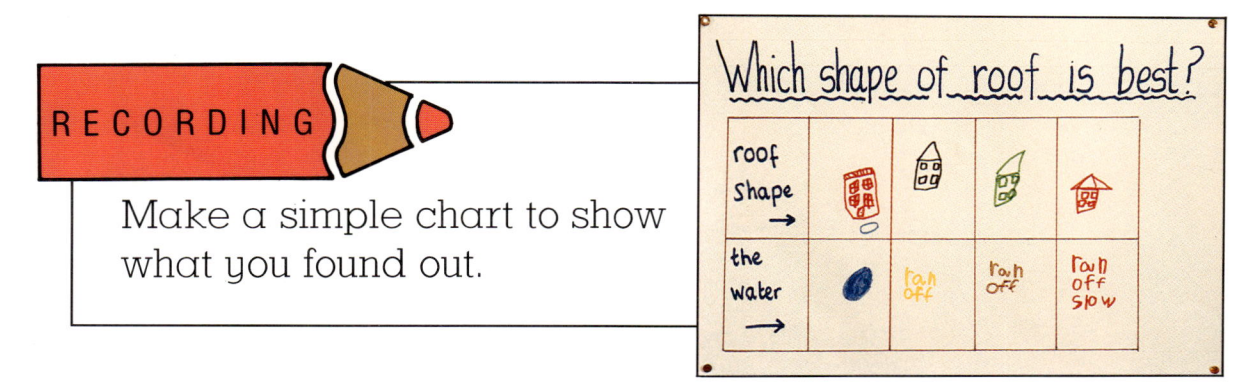

RECORDING

Make a simple chart to show what you found out.

11 TENTS

DESIGNING

Can you make up a story about living in a tent?
It could be:

- a wigwam
- an explorer's tent
- a tent at the bottom of a garden
- a tent in the desert

What are the best things about living in a tent?
What are the worst?
What adventures might you have?
Where would you cook your food?
How would you keep warm?
Who else might share your tent?

Draw some pictures to help tell your story.

Can you find some pictures of tents? You might find some in books, magazines or camping shop leaflets.
Copy the shapes onto a piece of paper or cut out the pictures.
How many different shapes of tent can you find?
Are they all the same size?
How many people do you think would fit in each one?

Making tent shapes

YOU NEED

Plastic straws   Pipe-cleaners   Glue
Sticky tape   Scissors   Fabric pieces
String

ACTIVITY -A-

Make some frames for tents. You could use straws or pipe-cleaners or a mixture of both. You could make one of these shapes:

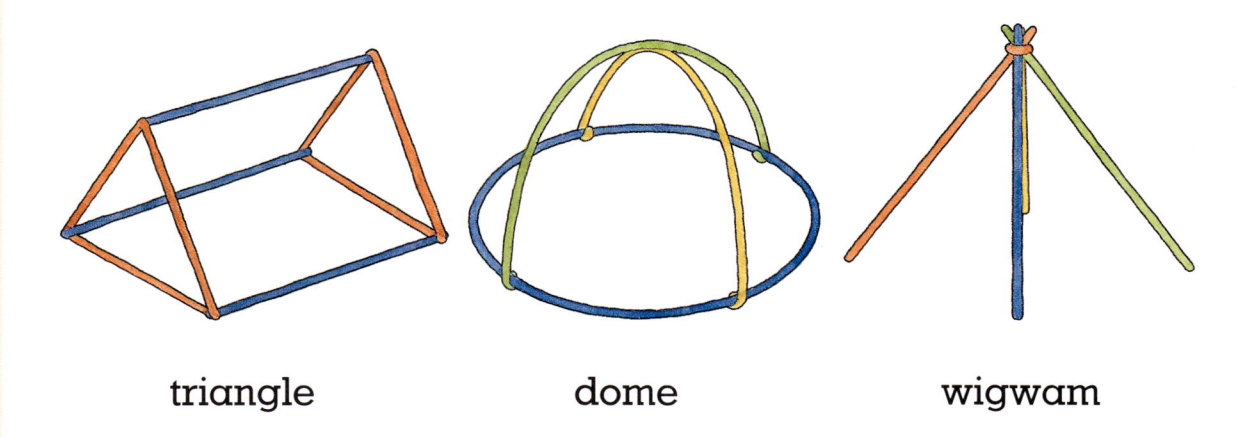

triangle   dome   wigwam

as well as ideas of your own.
Use glue or tape and string to hold the shapes together.
Cover the frames with pieces of cloth.

ACTIVITY -B-

Will your tent shapes stand up in a wind?
Try blowing them or you could use a bicycle or balloon pump.
Which shape is strongest?
You could make a tent village with your models.

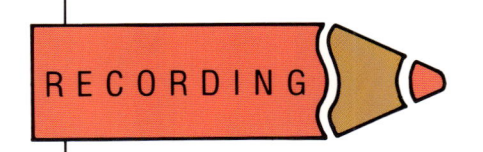

RECORDING

Photographs of the tents at frame and finished stages would make a good record. You could also draw the stages.

DESIGNING A HOUSE

Imagine that you are going to build a house. Think of the house which you would build. Will it have:
- a kitchen?
- a bathroom?
- a sitting room?
- a dining room?
- a play room?
- a garage?
- bedrooms?

How many rooms will it have altogether?
Will it have stairs?
It might have something special like a swimming pool or a tower.
Who would you like to live with in your house?
Would you have any pets?
Think about where everyone will sleep.
Draw a picture of the house.

What would you do if you wanted to sell your house?
Look in the newspaper and find the pages with houses for sale on them. What do the advertisements say about the houses?
Can you make up an advertisement for the house you have designed? It might look something like this.

Making a model house

YOU NEED

Boxes   Card   Tubes   Glue   Tape
Crayons   Paint   Coloured Paper
Fabric pieces

ACTIVITY

Think about the shape of the house you would like to make and what you will need to make it with.

Draw a picture of the house that you would like to make. At the side of the picture draw all the things which you will need to make the house.

Collect all the materials you will need and start building. When you have built the house does it look as you had planned? Did you copy your picture or did you need to change anything?

Draw a picture of your finished model and look at your two pictures together. Are they the same?

RECORDING

You can stick your pictures in your project book or make a class display of them.

13   WHAT IS INSIDE A HOUSE?

INVESTIGATING

When a house is built you need a lot of things before you are ready to live in it.
Think about the things you would need.
Think about:

carpets

curtains

wallpaper and paint

furniture

baths, sinks, toilets

cookers, fridges

washing machines

plates, cups, bowls

sheets, pillows and quilts

pans, spoons, knives and forks

as well as your own ideas.

Make a picture shopping list of everything you might need for your bedroom. Write or draw pictures for a story about getting your room ready.

Sharon's bedroom shopping list.

Finding out about things that you have in a home

YOU NEED
Paper   Pencils   Glue   Scissors
Books or magazine pictures

Think about your room or use the home corner or find some pictures of rooms in books or magazines.
Look at the things in the room.
What do you think they are made of?
Can you find:
- cloth?
- wood?
- plastic?
- metal?
- rubber?

What else can you find?

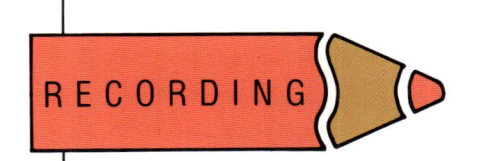

RECORDING

Look at your room and tick on a chart each time you find something made of one of the materials. Which material is used the most? Look at what your friends have found out. You could cut out some pictures of things and stick them on a chart.

14 STRONG HOUSES

INVESTIGATING

Think about the outside of your house.
What happens to it when it:
- rains? • snows? • is windy? • is sunny?

Why do we have to keep painting parts of our homes?
What happens to houses which are left empty for a long time?
Why do they get damaged and start to crumble?

What jobs have to be done to keep buildings in good repair? Think about new doors and windows, painting, mending broken tiles or roofs as well as your own ideas.

Tell a story about a deserted house. Perhaps some animals and birds live there.

Finding out about how different building materials wear

YOU NEED
A collection of building materials
Water in a bowl   Hammers   Sandpaper
Plastic bags

ACTIVITY -A-

Find out what happens when the building materials get wet.
First feel and look at the materials then put them in the bowl of water.
Have they changed colour?
Are there any bubbles?
Have they got heavier or lighter?
Take them out. How quickly do they dry?

ACTIVITY -B-

Find out how strong the materials are.
Rub them with sandpaper.
Do they make dust easily?
Do they wear down quickly?
Hit them with hammers.
Do they crumble easily?

What else could you do?
You might like to try putting them in the fridge.

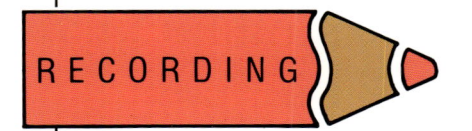

RECORDING

You could make a chart to show your results.

Acknowledgements

Copyright © 1990 Linda Howe
Reprinted 1991
ISBN 0 00 317547 2

Published by Collins Educational London and Glasgow
A division of HarperCollins

Design by David Bennett Books Ltd.
Illustrations by Amelia Rosato and Sally Neave
Commissioned photography by Oliver Hatch
Picture Research by Nance Fyson and Gwenan Morgan

Typeset by Kalligraphic Design Ltd., Horley, Surrey
Printed and bound in Hong Kong

All rights reserved. No part of this book may be reproduced or transmitted in any form or by any means, without the prior permission of the publisher.

The publishers thank St. John's First and Middle School, Ealing, London and Woolpit County Primary School, Suffolk for their kind co-operation in the production of Collins Primary Science.

Photographs – The publisher would like to thank the following for permission to reproduce photographs.

Ace Photo Agency 4tlc, 4br, 30; Ardea London Ltd 12tc, 12bc, 12br; Barnaby's Picture Library 4tr; Bruce Coleman Ltd 12tl; English Heritage 20t; Nance Fyson 4tl, 4bc; S & R Greenhill 4trc, 22t; Robert Harding Picture Library 4bl, 8tl, 8tr, 8br, 20b, 22b; Brian Shuel 8bl; Silvestris/NHPA 12bl

t = top, b = bottom, l = left, r = right, c = centre

Collins Primary Science

COLLINS PRIMARY SCIENCE is an activity-based science series for the primary school written by an experienced teacher *since* the publication of the National Curriculum. The series:
* is designed for use by all teachers whether science specialists or not
* fully covers all the attainment targets and statements of attainment contained in the National Curriculum
* provides scientific experiences within topics commonly taught in the primary school
* uses resources that are readily at hand
* provides a unique built-in assessment scheme

COLLINS PRIMARY SCIENCE consists of sets of ten books, grouped according to Key Stage. Each set has an accompanying Assessment Book and Teacher's Guide. The books in Key Stage 1 are designed to be used by a teacher and a group of children. Although many of the children will be unable to read the text for themselves, the books provide a shared opportunity for children and adults to find out about science together. The language of the books provides the perfect model for teachers to use when talking to children about science activities. The colour photographs and illustrations provide good talking points and will stimulate interest and invoke curiosity.

Collins Primary Science Key Stage 1 consists of two sets of ten books:

KEY STAGE 1, SET ONE	KEY STAGE 1, SET TWO
Drinks	Fruit and Vegetables
Soap and Washing	Clothing
Houses and Homes	Harvest and Hallowe'en
Wet and Dry	Stories
Colours	My School
Moving Things	Shops and Shopping
Our Senses	About Me
Nursery Rhymes	Water
Special Days	Toys
Eggs	Holes
0 00 317522 7	0 00 317523 5

Set One Assessment Book
— Helping with the Picnic
0 00 317549 9

Set Two Assessment Book
— The Adventures of a Space Visitor
0 00 317550 2

Teacher's Guide
0 00 317525 1

Teacher's Guide
0 00 317526 X

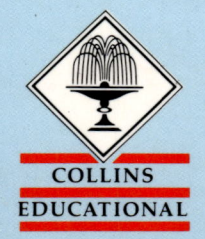

Collins Educational

ISBN 0-00-317547-2

KICKSTART

KS

Interactive - Leader's Manual

Ruth Lewis